Hidden Voices:
Older People's Experience
of Abuse

Written by Action on Elder Abuse and published by Help the Aged

Action on Elder Abuse
Astral House
1268 London Road
London
SW16 4ER

Registered charity no 1048397

Acknowledgements

The helpline has received financial support from
Comic Relief
Community Fund
Coutts
Goldsmiths' Charity
Ernest Kleinwort Charitable Trust
Hugh Fraser Foundation
Lloyd's TSB Foundation
Robertson Foundation
Sobell Foundation

There are also a significant number of individuals and organisations that regularly contribute to the funding of the helpline but do not wish to receive publicity. We are most grateful to these contributors.

The views and recommendations contained within this report are those of the authors and do not necessarily reflect the opinions of individual funding bodies.

About the author

Written by Gary FitzGerald, Chief Executive of Action on Elder Abuse, with contributions from Sue Grant, Peter Westland, Tessa Harding, Stephen Ladyman, Bridget Penhale, Jill Manthorpe and Dr Paul Kingston.

ISBN: 1-904528-80-5

Published by Help the Aged. A CIP record for this book is available from the British Library.

A note from Help the Aged

This report from Action on Elder Abuse (AEA) is an important contribution to our understanding of elder abuse. Drawing upon the evidence of nearly 7,000 calls to the AEA helpline since 1997, it explores both the extent and the varied nature of the abuse itself and the policy and conceptual context that govern how society responds to it.

There is an uncomfortable contrast between the convulsion of public soul-searching that follows such appalling cases as the death of Victoria Climbié and the lack of public attention given to cases of older people who have suffered equally devastating injuries, either by deliberate commission or by neglect. Yet as the report points out, an average of 35 cases of abuse of older people are reported every month in local newspapers, often with a real sense of shock and horror that such things can happen.

The Government intends to establish a new Commission for Equality and Human Rights by early 2007. The commission will have powers to promote and enforce anti-discrimination law and to encourage good equality practice in a broad range of areas, including age. We know that age discrimination is widespread and can affect many aspects of older people's lives (Help the Aged 2004). There is a link between such discrimination and the abuse of human rights.

'Beginning to see elders as objects rather than human is the foundation on which a continuum of petty slights and abuses builds into active mistreatment' (Biggs, Phillipson and Kingston 1995). It is this 'objectifying' of older people that denies them their role as participating citizens and their right to control over their own lives, whatever their circumstances.

The new commission will also be charged with promoting human rights. The Human Rights Act 1998 should ensure that people's right to life is respected and that they are free from inhuman and degrading treatment. It spells out rights to privacy and respect for personal and family life and the right to the peaceful enjoyment of one's possessions. These rights are universal and should underpin the way public services are provided. To date, there is little evidence to show that public services have taken the Human Rights Act to heart (Audit Commission 2003). The role of the new commission, alongside the bodies responsible for training, regulating and inspecting those services, will therefore be crucial.

We believe the new commission should be able to take action to enforce human rights, where necessary. It is not enough to say that older people can themselves take legal action in defence of their human rights when we know that those who suffer abuse are rarely in a position to challenge the way they are treated. A sense of powerlessness, lack of knowledge and support, and fear all contribute to making it extremely difficult for older people (or indeed others) to challenge abusive treatment.

This report provides a much-needed opportunity to extend our knowledge and understanding of abuse. It complements the powerful report from the Health Select Committee on Elder Abuse in April 2004. Together these should mark a turning point and bring elder abuse out of the closet of society's guilty secrets and on to the political agenda. We will need a comprehensive programme of action if we are to tackle the complexities of elder abuse and ensure that older people enjoy their human rights free from fear of harm or neglect.

Tessa Harding
Senior Policy Advisor
September 2004

Foreword

The abuse of older people cannot be tolerated. That is why the Department

quickly and effectively with those who perpetrate abuse.

When reading this report, I urge you all to think beyond the statistics and focus on the human suffering resulting from abuse. There should be no doubt that the abuse of vulnerable adults is a scar on our society. There should be no hiding place for professionals and other carers who betray the trust placed in them.

I congratulate Action on Elder Abuse for this report and for its tireless campaigning for the rights of vulnerable adults.

phen Ladyman
liamentary Under Secretary of State
Community
partment of Health

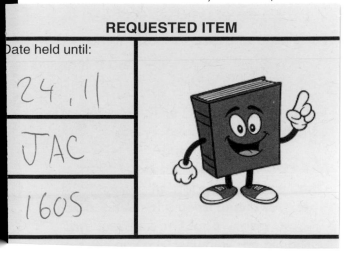
MERTHYR LOANS

MAXIMUM RENEWAL PERIODS

1 WEEK LOAN 10 WEEKS

4 WEEK LOAN 16 WEEKS

HIGH DEMAND 1 WEEK

PLEASE MONITOR YOUR

EMAILS CAREFULLY FOR

ANY RECALLS ON YOUR

BOOKS, FINES WILL BE

CHARGED FOR LATE RETURNS.

Contents

Summary and recommendations

1 Introduction

The prime focus of Action on Elder Abuse (AEA) since it was established in 1993 has been to increase awareness and understanding of the abuse of older people, who are often some of the least-protected members of society.

Elder Abuse Response, the national telephone helpline run by AEA, was set up in 1997 following a successful pilot project. Run by specially trained staff and volunteers, the helpline provides free, confidential information and advice to members of the public, students and practitioners. The service has taken more than 10,000 calls.

AEA has now carried out an analysis of all the calls received in the last six-and-a-half years, providing further evidence concerning the existence, extent and nature of elder abuse in the UK.

2 The role and purpose of the helpline: putting it all in context

Neglect and mistreatment of older people are not rare events but occur in places that we term 'care' settings and are carried out by those whom we term carers or those who have a duty of care.

It is evident that abuse and mistreatment are not 'simply' the result of 'evil' relations or staff preying on vulnerable older people. The calls to the helpline suggest that it is more complicated and that responsibility for abuse lies at many levels, as does responsibility for improving matters.

3 Scope of data collection and reporting

An analysis of calls to the Elder Abuse Response helpline has been undertaken on three separate occasions, since it was established six-and-a-half years ago in 1997. This is the third occasion and, like the previous two, shows that an older person may suffer from one or several different types of abuse at the same time, that the abuser can be a fellow resident (if in a care setting or sheltered housing), and that racial abuse manifests itself in the standard five categories of abuse.

4 Who contacts the helpline?

Overall, women are three times more likely to call the helpline than men (a ratio of 76:24).

Despite the existence of the Public Interest Disclosure Act 1998, it is not the experience of AEA that this has created a culture in which social and health care employees feel able to disclose abuse.

It is important to recognise that the two most numerous groups who contact the helpline are relatives and older people themselves — indicating a greater willingness to take action than may previously have been recognised.

ADVICE TO INDIVIDUALS

4.1 Sometimes it can be difficult to pursue your concerns, but do not give up. Achieving a successful outcome might take time but it is worth it, so keep raising concerns until you are satisfied.

4.2 Ask questions if you are concerned and challenge issues if they appear to be wrong. Use complaints procedures and contact the relevant regulator to make your views known. Keep records of everything you see, the names of people you speak to, and when, and copies of any letters you write.

4.3 Publicise the existence of the Elder Abuse Response helpline (tel: **0808 808 8141**). An increase in the number of people who know how to contact us for support will help to raise awareness of the issue.

RECOMMENDATIONS FOR STATUTORY/ORGANISATIONAL GROUPS

4.4 The existence of complaints procedures should be given greater publicity by statutory and regulatory bodies, and by providers themselves, and active consideration should be given to the use of advocates as a matter of general good practice.

4.5 The effect of the Public Interest Disclosure Act 1998 should be evaluated by an independent body to establish what further actions need to be considered, including legislative actions, to ensure greater use within social and health care services.

5 Definitions and types of elder abuse

The AEA definition of elder abuse is:

A single or repeated act or lack of appropriate action occurring within any relationship where there is an expectation of trust, which causes harm or distress to an older person.

AEA identifies abuse in five primary categories: physical, psychological, financial, sexual and neglect, and gives examples of such abuse from media reports. It indicates that the type of abuse most frequently reported to the helpline is psychological (34 per cent), followed by financial abuse (20 per cent)

and physical abuse (19 per cent) in almost equal numbers. Neglect is reported at 12 per cent, while sexual abuse is identified in 3 per cent of cases. There is a high percentage of multiple abuses, with 44 per cent of callers reporting more than one type of abuse occurring simultaneously.

ADVICE TO INDIVIDUALS

5.1 Think about the impact of psychological abuse – how hard it is to spot, and what a major impact it can have on an older person. Have you unintentionally placed pressure on someone to do something – or not do something – by suggesting it would have implications (for example, denying a visit by grandchildren or continued help with personal care)? Casual suggestions can have major implications for someone who is dependent upon you, so always make sure that your intentions are clear and, if you are drawing attention to the implications of an action, always make sure it is done in the right way, ie it is not seen as a threat.

5.2 Abuse can sometimes be subtle and it is not always easy to spot the signs. Download a copy of the factsheet from the AEA website and learn about the differing types of abuse and how they can be spotted.

5.3 Neglect has a physical impact. If perpetrated by a service provider, it can also cause psychological distress to relatives and friends (if, for example, the neglect leads to serious conditions such as pressure sores).

RECOMMENDATIONS FOR STATUTORY/ORGANISATIONAL GROUPS

5.4 All powers of attorney should be the subject of recording and control, with two levels of registration: (a) those that have been established but are not yet in force; and (b) those that are in force either due to lack of capacity by the vulnerable person, or where a witnessed decision has been taken to bring them into force earlier.

5.5 The current limited status of unregistered powers of attorney should be given greater publicity, particularly within high-risk groups.

5.6 The appropriate regulatory bodies, and professional bodies, should undertake a publicity and information campaign to highlight good nursing and care practice in relation to pressure sores, and the development of such sores should be considered a primary indicator of neglect or poor care practice and receive an appropriately serious response.

6 Who are the abusers?

More men are reported as individual abusers (41 per cent) than women (25 per cent). Overwhelmingly, male abusers are family members (64 per cent). But while this is equally true for women (51 per cent), there is also a significant proportion (33 per cent) of female abusers identified as paid staff.

In a third of circumstances, the abuse is perpetrated by more than one person in collusion. Although 23 per cent of this collusive abuse is perpetrated by family members, a staggering 62 per cent is perpetrated by paid staff – that is, through abusive practices that are institutional and passed from one worker to another.

Although more men than woman are identified as abusers, 33 per cent of abuse is perpetrated by men and women at the same time (with the majority of this being institutional poor practice). The majority of abusers are related to their victim (46 per cent), while paid workers are the next highest category (34 per cent). However, we are unable to support the hypothesis that the stress of informal (unpaid) caring by family members leads to abusive practices. While it is accepted that such caring can be intensely stressful, we receive less than 1 per cent of calls identifying these carers as abusers.

ADVICE TO INDIVIDUALS

6.1 Unfortunately, you must learn to believe the unbelievable. Vulnerable older people get abused in the UK today. Accepting that fact increases the possibility of your spotting when something goes wrong, and when something does not feel right.

6.2 If you have suspicions, tell someone. Share your concerns and make an adult protection referral to your local authority, if you live in England or Wales; if you live in Ireland or Scotland, ring our helpline for advice.

6.3 Care workers should never fall into the trap of going along with peer group activity that seems to betray trust. If it feels wrong, then it probably is wrong and you will regret it later if abuse becomes the consequence of turning a blind eye. Talk to us, or to your trade union. But, whatever you do, don't do nothing.

RECOMMENDATIONS FOR STATUTORY/ORGANISATIONAL GROUPS

6.4 A task force should be established, comprising regulators, providers and voluntary sector groups, to evaluate trends and patterns of abuse within care provision (both health and social care) and to recommend changes or improvements in current guidance, regulation or commissioning practice as appropriate.

6.5 A major publicity campaign should be funded by the Government to highlight elder abuse – primarily but not exclusively targeted toward abuse within families – to reinforce the message that it is unacceptable within society.

7 Who are the victims?

The vast majority of those who are reported as suffering abuse are women (67 per cent) with 22 per cent of men identified as victims. In a smaller percentage of cases (11 per cent), both men and women are facing abuse at the same time, and more than half of these (50 per cent) are in some form of institution, primarily care homes.

The fact that more women than men are identified as suffering abuse is likely to reflect the reality that women live longer than men and are consequently more likely to be living alone. It may also be that men are less likely to report being abused.

More than three-quarters of abuse (78 per cent) is perpetrated against people who are over the age of 70, with 16 per cent of that abuse affecting people over the age of 90. For both men and women, it appears that the period between 80 and 89 years of age is the time of most vulnerability to abuse.

ADVICE TO INDIVIDUALS

7.1 A potential victim can be the older person living alone without active friends or relatives, or the older person always alone in the care home. Isolation gives opportunity for abuse, so a simple way of reducing

that possibility is to keep in touch with family and friends. Simply stay in touch, and let the people around the older person know that you are doing so.

7.2 Always remember that abuse is no respecter of social or financial status. You can become a victim whether you are very well-off or are living on a state pension.

7.3 Try to look at more than what is obvious. Gentle interest in someone's circumstances is different from prying, but it might uncover issues of concern. Try to do more than just listening to what is said to you. Hear it and think. Sometimes people find strange ways of telling you they have a problem, and you have to hear beyond the words in order to understand.

RECOMMENDATIONS FOR STATUTORY/ORGANISATIONAL GROUPS

7.4 Ensure that any adult protection strategies take account of the viewpoint of older victims, together with an understanding of their history and identity. They lived through different times and have different perceptions. That needs to be recognised.

8 Settings of abuse

Most abuse occurs in people's own homes (64 per cent). This is not surprising as it is where the majority of older people live and where it is very difficult to monitor and prevent abuse.

However, 23 per cent of reports to the helpline concern care homes (formerly known as residential and nursing homes), where less than 5 per cent of the older population live. This is a disproportionate figure, made starker by the reality that callers need to be able to access a telephone in private – something that is not always easy in a care home.

Hospital settings account for 5 per cent of all calls while sheltered housing accounts for 4 per cent.

In simplistic terms, it would be possible to suggest that financial and psychological abuses could be associated with domiciliary settings, while psychological abuse and neglect could be associated with institutions.

ADVICE TO INDIVIDUALS

8.1 Make a note to periodically call on older neighbours, friends or family members, and try to do it at different times so that other people do not know when you are calling. This simple action can prevent abuse, as those with limited social contact with other people are more vulnerable.

8.2 Do not rely on service providers, the local authority or regulators to ensure that your friend or your family member is safe. Regardless of standards or inspection or anything else, you should seek to ensure for yourself that everything is all right.

RECOMMENDATIONS FOR STATUTORY/ORGANISATIONAL GROUPS

8.3 Abuse by families should be the subject of a publicity and awareness-raising campaign similar to that undertaken within the domestic violence arena. Elder abuse is a hate crime and it needs to be perceived as such.

9 The four nations

From the perspective of responding to sensitive personal issues such as elder abuse, it is important to consider and understand the background, history and culture of people in order to provide appropriate support. Comparative data for the four nations of the UK, as well as Ireland, is provided. However, although the data is limited, there is some evidence that the nature of abuse can vary across the four nations.

ADVICE TO INDIVIDUALS

9.1 Being a minority within a wider community can result in isolation, and this can result in abuse. It is too easy to stereotype individuals and make assumptions about what their family may or may not do for them. Check to make sure that what you think is happening is based on reality.

9.2 Although it is important not to stereotype and not to make racist assumptions, it is just as important to question, and, where necessary, challenge if something appears to be wrong. But be sensitive to culture, religion and identity.

9.3 While it is important for all the nations within the UK to be proud of their unique cultures and identities, it is also important to recognise that some issues transcend nationality. The abuse of older people is a blight, no matter where it occurs, and nothing should impede our joint desire to challenge and eliminate it. Consequently, there is a responsibility upon all governments, assemblies and peoples to work together, and share knowledge and advice wherever it may originate from. Ask yourself whether you are operating from that perspective and, if not, think about why.

RECOMMENDATIONS FOR STATUTORY/ORGANISATIONAL GROUPS

9.4 Minority ethnic advocates on elder abuse should be identified, trained and available.

9.5 The Scottish Parliament and the Northern Irish and Welsh Assemblies should consider establishing formal inquiries into the nature and extent of elder abuse within their nations.

10 Perceptions that influence our understanding of elder abuse

In considering perceptions of abuse, it is important to look at concepts of crime and ageing, what constitutes abuse itself, and the nature of citizenship. It is also important to question the lesser position of older people within society and the differing responses toward elder abuse.

In avoiding or ignoring the issue of criminality, we fall into the danger of colluding in the discrimination against an older person and, in so doing, of leaving them outside of ordinary civil and human rights. Since older people are 'constructed' as both dependent and a burden, it implies that society has developed a feeling that all people over 65 years need care. However, citizenship seeks to reinforce the mutual obligations (between individual and society) inherent in social inclusion policies, rather than regard vulnerable older people as primarily clients and patients needing protection.

ADVICE TO INDIVIDUALS

10.1 Older people have the same rights now as they did when they were younger. Think about your approach and the assumptions that you make. To what extent might your actions take away their rights to choice and control – whether or not your actions are based upon good intentions? Do you help people achieve a quality of life, or simply an existence?

RECOMMENDATIONS FOR STATUTORY/ORGANISATIONAL GROUPS

10.2 Advice should be issued to police forces clarifying the advantages of implementing vulnerable witness strategies for anyone who has been the victim of elder abuse (as defined by the AEA definition and categories).

10.3 The use of the Regina vs Stone & Dobinson case law should be brought to the attention of the Crown Prosecution Service (CPS) and all police forces and encouragement be given to its active use in situations that appear to indicate wilful neglect.

10.4 A review should be undertaken of the decisions of the CPS taken in the last two years where elder abuse cases have not been pursued because prosecution was felt not to be 'in the public interest', and guidance should subsequently be devised and issued.

10.5 Legislation should be drafted that criminalises the neglect of or cruelty towards an adult.

10.6 An urgent exploration should be undertaken into the most appropriate legal terminology to adequately define a 'vulnerable adult', including circumstances in which vulnerability does not arise solely through a lack of mental capacity.

10.7 Full compliance with the relevant articles of the Human Rights Act should be made a pre-condition of registration of care services under the Care Standards Act (as proposed by Help the Aged).

11 Theoretical models and risk factors

Academics and practitioners have sought to identify certain predisposing factors within abusive situations. These include:

- Intra-individual dynamics – for example, mental health problems or alcohol dependency.

- Inter-generational transmission of violence An extension of domestic violence into older age, or children of previously abusive parents turning the violence against their dependent mother or father.

- Dependency This multi-tiered and complicated issue requires careful consideration in any social or health care assessment (including carers' needs assessment).

- Stress of caring Our helpline analysis indicates that only 1 per cent of calls are about abuse perpetrated by a primary carer.

- Social isolation 36 per cent of those living in care homes and 19 per cent of those living in private households are rarely visited by relatives or friends, with 6 per cent of care home residents and 2 per cent of those living at home receiving no visits at all (Department of Health 2000a).

There are a number of other theoretical models for risk factors: for example, 'abuser deviance', pathological family cultures and power imbalance. However, the problem with lists of risk factors is that they can rarely be comprehensive, so the aim should always be to ask questions about the lives, support needs and choices of the individuals involved.

Good adult protection occurs when information, behaviour or clues are not judged simply on the basis of 'tick boxes' or 'prejudices' but upon assessment of the individual in totality.

12 Successful interventions

- Underlying principles We believe it is necessary to start from the premise that prevention is always better than intervention and that this approach should be inherent in adult protection policies and procedures. Also, the dynamics of family-related elder abuse are often similar to those within domestic violence settings.

- Collaborative working Successful adult protection requires multi-layered strategies that operate simultaneously. It also needs co-ordination between agencies, the sharing of information, and a willingness to seek expert advice from others.

- Developing unique strategies It is not appropriate simply to import child protection strategies into adult protection. Adults with capacity have choice, and while they may be frail and vulnerable, they have the right to exercise that choice. We need to think creatively about this area and do much more work to develop strategies that are relevant to adults.

- Addressing poor practice: training The experience of the AEA helpline is that poor practice forms the greatest percentage of abuse perpetrated by paid staff. Consequently, we strongly promote appropriate training – both practical and theoretical, and for everyone involved in the sector – as one guaranteed method of reducing the potential for such abuse.

- Addressing poor practice: culture We believe that the culture of an organisation can encourage abuse. Maintaining a positive culture can be effected only by good training and good supervision, and setting realistic standards, monitoring them and reacting accordingly. We also need to create a general climate where it is acceptable to question and challenge without repercussions.

- Empowerment We also need to look closely at what constitutes genuine empowerment. Research into adult protection in England at the beginning of 2003 showed that the vast majority of local authorities had met their statutory responsibility in establishing procedures (97 per cent). But they had failed miserably to publicise the existence of those procedures (Centre for Policy on Ageing 2003). Less than 2 per cent had invested in systems to tell people about adult protection.

- Whistle-blowing We believe that whistle-blowing can be a crucial component in strategies to combat abuse. But this will happen only when whistle-blowing itself becomes integrated into the wider philosophies of good practice, codes of conduct and expected activities – that is, when professional bodies perceive a failure to 'blow the whistle' as an unacceptable breach of their codes of conduct.

ADVICE TO INDIVIDUALS

12.1 Think about what steps you can take to prevent the possibility of abuse occurring, or recurring. Have you tried to reduce the potential for abuse by changing the way services are delivered or the manner in which care is provided?

Try to introduce transparency into activities so that actions are obvious.

12.2 Think about what we have learned from domestic violence experiences; why people do not always recognise themselves as victims or readily accept options for protection. Think about the relationship between mothers/fathers and their children in that context.

12.3 Consider to what extent professional rivalries within your organisation might get in the way of asking for assistance, or the degree to which the Data Protection Act 1998 is seen as a barrier to information-sharing. Have the lessons from the Bichard Inquiry, or the Harold Shipman or Victoria Climbié Inquiries, had an impact on what you are doing?

12.4 Consider what training you have received or given, to assist a greater understanding of elder abuse. Talk to AEA about the training currently on offer, or that could be developed for your organisation.

12.5 What culture operates within your organisation? For example, if you are in residential care, do you consider it to be a care home or a hotel for older people? If you are in domiciliary care, do you provide services to numbers of people or are they individuals? And if you are at home, do you resent the time your partner gives to caring for her mother, or is it something you recognise as worthwhile?

12.6 Get a copy of the reports of the Harold Shipman inquiry and ensure colleagues read the parts where the failure to challenge a GP allowed him to kill hundreds of innocent people. Could it happen again?

12.7 Consider how safe or easy it is for you or a colleague, or a member of your staff, to whistle-blow. What needs to change to make it easier? How would you find out if abuse was being hidden from you?

RECOMMENDATIONS FOR STATUTORY/ORGANISATIONAL GROUPS

12.8 Mandatory training should be given to health and social care staff with regard to the nature of elder abuse, the warning signs and what action can be taken. This training should be available to hospital and primary care teams, including district nurses and ancillary staff.

13 About research: a context for the helpline

Research into elder abuse is limited, which makes it easy for the extent of the problem to be underestimated – which is unlikely to be reflected within a child protection debate. However, although information overall is relatively slight, taken collectively, it implies a level of abuse that is significant.

RECOMMENDATIONS FOR STATUTORY/ORGANISATIONAL GROUPS

13.1 A national research strategy should be established within which researchers are encouraged or commissioned to operate.

13.2 Focused research should be commissioned to establish the factors contributing to elder abuse within minority ethnic communities.

13.3 A comprehensive prevalence study should be commissioned by the relevant governments and assemblies to establish the extent and impact of elder abuse throughout the UK.

1 Introduction

Elder Abuse Response, the national helpline run by Action on Elder Abuse (AEA), was established in 1997 following a successful pilot project which was held in a number of different areas of the UK. The pilot project was set up in 1995 in order to provide information about elder abuse and also to provide support, advice and information to callers who were making contact because they were concerned about specific incidents of abuse or suspected abuse. The pilot ran for 12 months and an evaluation of the helpline and calls received during this period indicated there was an unmistakable need for a specialised national helpline on elder abuse.

Once funding was secure, the national helpline was established and is provided by AEA using staff and volunteers who have undertaken specific training for this purpose. The helpline operates at different levels: as a free-phone service for members of the public and for practitioners working with older people. The confidential service provides information and support to callers, helps people identify possible options for action, and also discusses raising concerns with care organisations and providers as well as with statutory bodies. Information about elder abuse is provided by telephone, letter or, increasingly, by email. The service has now taken more than 10,000 calls, including requests for information about abuse from practitioners, students and the general public.

However, in the light of a number of initiatives at national level in recent years, including the Health Committee Single Evidence Hearing on Elder Abuse, which took place 2003-4, it was necessary to re-evaluate the helpline service and to analyse the calls received in the last six-and-a-half year. The Chief Executive and staff members of AEA were actively involved in work on this for over four months. This report documents the findings of their careful and painstaking work.

The prime focus of AEA's work since it was established in 1993 has been to educate professionals and the public about elder abuse and to encourage individuals to think carefully about actions and behaviours taken towards older people, who are often some of the least protected members of society. Through the work of the helpline, the charity is now reaching a public audience that increasingly wishes to know what elder abuse is, what can be done to help, how to react to difficult, complex and often impossible situations and what sort of interventions can be achieved. The analysis of calls is of additional value in that it provides further evidence concerning the existence and nature of abuse in the UK. As one of the charity's first trustees and a current member of the advisory group for Action on Elder Abuse, I am delighted that the report of the helpline analysis, *Hidden Voices*, is now being launched. The report, together with its detailed findings, serves as a platform to take us forward in our work to combat elder abuse in all its forms.

Bridget Penhale
Senior Lecturer
Department of Community, Ageing, Rehabilitation, Education and Research
School of Nursing and Midwifery
University of Sheffield

2 The role and purpose of the helpline: putting it all in context

This report makes sad reading. It confirms that neglect and mistreatment of older people are not rare events but occur in places that we term 'care' settings and are carried out by those whom we term carers or those who have a duty of care. Are matters getting worse? Is there an epidemic of abuse? Do we discriminate against older people in ways which would be totally unacceptable for other groups?

Answers to some of these questions are contained in this report. It is evident that abuse and mistreatment are not 'simply' the result of 'evil' relations or staff preying on vulnerable older people. The calls to the helpline suggest that it is all more complicated and that responsibility for abuse lies at many levels, but so too does responsibility for improving matters. It is now evident that, increasingly, older people and their relatives recognise that poor care or abusive relationships require action. Over two-thirds of the callers to the helpline are older people themselves or their family members.

We are not able to say that abuse is increasing – only that it appears to be more widely recognised. This is one key achievement of organisations such as Action on Elder Abuse – they have raised awareness among professionals but they are also inspiring older people and their families to confront abusive situations.

So, although there is no evidence for an epidemic of abuse, it is useful perhaps to suggest the metaphor that confidence that something can be done is contagious. It would be useful also if future reports could include information about the outcomes of calls to the helpline – although the difficulties of obtaining these are acknowledged.

A report on outcomes would help us tease out the reality of 'discriminatory abuse'. Current and recent calls to the helpline suggest that inadequate care is one category that evokes great concern, and rightly so. Is this, in fact, discrimination? Does it mean that standards and expectations for older people are significantly lower or different than for other groups? One potential use of such a report could be to help us think about this knotty subject.

Ever since the Action on Elder Abuse helpline opened, there have been many occasions on which I have referred people to it. I have spoken of its existence to students, many of whom did not know it existed but numbers of whom have been dismayed by what they have seen happening to older people in health and social care settings. Despite their independence, enthusiasm, and the backing of a higher education institution, students often feel uncertain about what to do and where to turn. If they have not made use of it, I hope knowing that the helpline exists will help them to raise concerns and to provide the type of care they want to deliver.

Second, I have found practitioners, in all settings, find the existence of a helpline that is expert in this area to be a source of assistance – both real and potential. It is all too easy for practitioners to be told 'tell your manager', but sometimes their manager cannot help, and sadly, at times, will not.

Third, the helpline's existence is a key resource to publicise to anyone with an interest in promoting the rights of older people. This general phrase does not always have much meaning but it really underlines what people are talking about when they start to tell you a story about someone they know and what is happening to them.

These three potential users of the helpline need to know that they will be met with a 'listening ear'. They need to know that they will receive accurate advice, based on the real world rather than some idealised state. They need to know that this advice is aware of local sources of help, and their limitations.

So this report provides evidence that, across the UK, people are contacting the helpline with these types of concerns. Rather than dramatising the individual accounts, this report takes the opportunity to think about what is happening.

This report is not sensationalising. It recognises that there are many causes and definitions of abuse and that we need simultaneously to prevent abuse and to promote the rights of older people. Often this will involve promoting the rights and welfare of those who provide support in paid or family roles.

The report flags up for me, as someone with a keen interest in the social care workforce, the ongoing need for training, good working conditions and cultures that respect vulnerable people. Paid staff now form about one-third of the helpline's callers, so it is timely perhaps to think about further ways to encourage their calls and to develop other channels that can link their concerns to action at local levels.

Finally, a word about the helpline volunteers. It is not easy to give support over the telephone, not knowing if the advice is helpful, sometimes talking to people in distress. But volunteers are the backbone of the helpline. They deserve our thanks for their commitment, enthusiasm and skills.

Jill Manthorpe
Social Care Workforce Research Unit
King's College London
Chair: Hull and East Riding Adult
Protection Committee

3 Scope of data collection and reporting

An analysis of calls to the Elder Abuse Response helpline has been undertaken on three separate occasions. In 1997, we published an interim analysis of 315 calls (Action on Elder Abuse 1997). This was followed in February 2000 by an analysis of 1,421 calls (Action on Elder Abuse 2000). More recent data, covering 6,867 calls, is now available and is quoted in this report.

In considering the report, it is important to note that:

a) while the number of calls evaluated increased from 315 to 6,867, all of the analyses have returned a consistent picture in terms of the nature of elder abuse;

b) the information has been gathered only from those able or willing to use a telephone helpline;

c) as the figures reflect, an older person may either suffer from only one type of abuse or from different types of abuse at the same time, and the abuse may occur in more than one setting;

d) in calls about abuse in care settings or sheltered housing, a few were about abuse by fellow residents. When recording details of these calls, the person subjected to the abuse was categorised as the abused and the resident committing the abuse as the abuser;

e) decisions about whether or not an incident was indeed abusive were made by individual helpline operators, who also categorised those involved as either 'abused' (victim) or 'abuser' (perpetrator) based on their expertise and judgment of the information given. Their categorisation of practitioners' occupations, family members' relationships and places where abuse occurred was also based on information given by callers. There has been no attempt to verify the categorisations independently;

f) due to the confidential nature of the helpline, and the difficulties inherent in guiding and supporting callers who are often in distress, it has not yet been possible to establish a process whereby ethnic monitoring data can be sensitively obtained. However, it has been our experience that racial abuse usually manifests itself in one of the standard five categories of abuse detailed in Chapter 4;

g) the helpline operators are skilled in identifying a call in which there is doubt or uncertainty about the content of the call or the motivation of the caller – an ex-employee, perhaps, who harbours a grudge or a family member who is unhappy with a collective family decision. However, 85 per cent of all abuse calls contain sufficient information to be classed as demonstrable abuse; and

h) although, by its very nature, a helpline has certain limitations, the Elder Abuse Response helpline provides a unique insight into the nature of elder abuse in the UK.

4 Who contacts the helpline?

Overall, women are three times more likely to call the helpline than men (a ratio of 76:24).

The two most common types of callers are relatives of those who are receiving care or support (41 per cent) whether from a paid service or through unpaid family or alternative support, and older people themselves (27 per cent).

Traditionally, older people have been perceived as unwilling to complain (and many of the relatives who contact us are themselves over 65). Yet this level of contact suggests that they will use a service if it specialises in their needs and this indicates a greater willingness on their part to take action than may have been previously recognised.

Relatives and older people usually contact the helpline because they are unhappy about something that is happening or has happened, and they are unable to obtain change or redress through the immediate options available to them. In some cases, this is because they are not aware of their rights (for example, how to access complaints processes or regulatory bodies). In other cases, it is because they have failed to obtain a response that is acceptable to them. This is equally true for the friends/neighbours category of callers (11 per cent).

The next most common type of caller is paid workers (19 per cent). They typically contact the helpline because they have seen something or have been told to do something that concerns them, or because they are investigating a complaint/abuse referral and are seeking advice on options or legislation.

Often, when workers are seeking to report an abuse that they have witnessed, they are doing so with varying levels of anxiety and fear of the consequences for themselves. In our

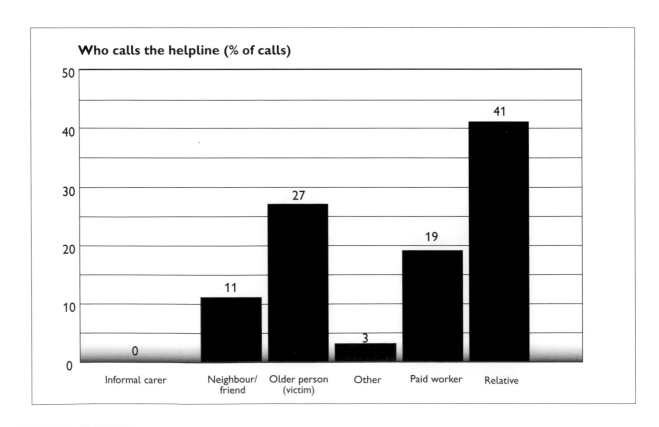

Who calls the helpline (% of calls)

Informal carer	Neighbour/ friend	Older person (victim)	Other	Paid worker	Relative
0	11	27	3	19	41

experience, the Public Interest Disclosure Act 1998 has not created a culture in which social and health care employees feel able to disclose abuse.

Indeed, it is still suggested that disclosure can lead to loss of employment and, in some cases, people have reported that they felt it necessary to move to another area. These pressures may be deliberate on the part of the employer. In other cases, however, the whistle-blower may simply feel unable to continue in that employment, particularly if they believe that the employer has not acted with sufficient resolve.

5 Definitions and types of elder abuse

Defining elder abuse

A single or repeated act or lack of appropriate action occurring within any relationship where there is an expectation of trust, which causes harm or distress to an older person.

This definition of elder abuse developed by AEA is very specific and is focused upon a breach of trust. This is important because it allows us to concentrate specifically on those abuses where it would be reasonable for the older person to have trusted the abuser (for example, relatives, staff who are employed to help them). As such, it excludes abuse perpetrated by strangers (for example, distraction burglary or mugging).

Our definition differs from that used in *No Secrets* (Department of Health 2000b), which covers only those older people who *'are or may be in need of community care services'* or who *'cannot take care of themselves'* or *'protect* [themselves] *from significant harm or exploitation'*.

By its nature, the *No Secrets* definition is based on a health/social care model – that is, it assumes that a vulnerable person must be in need of external support, and it ignores the emotional/psychological impact of an abusive relationship. This consequently discounts a range of abuses that are psychological in nature but that may not be readily definable as *'significant harm or exploitation'*.

Types of elder abuse

AEA identifies abuse in five primary categories. The italicised examples which follow are taken from local newspaper reports as illustrative (and actual) cases.

PHYSICAL ABUSE
Includes slapping, hitting, burning, head-butting, scalding, bruising, pushing, restraining, and the inappropriate administration of medicines (including withholding medication).

9 October 2003
Two nursing home owners who turned a blind eye to the widespread abuse of elderly residents for more than three years were struck off the nursing register. Allegations included one that the couple had themselves behaved inappropriately when they were seen 'restraining' a woman on the toilet by pulling the back of her dress up and over her face. Other abuses included a care assistant shaking the broken arm of a resident repeatedly to stop it healing quickly, and a staff member pulling chunks of hair from the head of another resident. Residents were taken to the toilet in mixed-sex groups without screens to protect their dignity. The couple were alleged to have taken no action in response to complaints by other members of staff and ordered members of staff not to record injuries to residents.

18 February 2001
Visitors were encouraged to ring ahead when they came to see relatives at the nursing home in Oxford. It gave the staff time to hide the stench of urine and scrape faeces off the curtains. Not that they would ever see the 89-year-old man whose suppurating pressure sores had rotted the flesh right down to his bones. He was locked away upstairs, in too much pain to move and too much confusion to cry out. For the last four months of his life he saw no one except the proprietor, who attempted to clean his wounds by hacking at the skin around the sores with office scissors and ripping out his rotting flesh, wearing gloves he had used to scoop faeces off the sheets moments earlier.

PSYCHOLOGICAL ABUSE
Includes shouting, swearing, frightening, blaming, threatening, intimidating, ignoring, humiliating, and using threats of denying a person access to something – a person, pet, object or activity – that they enjoy, value or love.

11 June 2003
A nurse accused of running a care home like a military 'boot camp' escaped being struck off the nursing register despite being found guilty of abusing mentally ill residents. At a hearing last October, the Nursing and Midwifery Council heard that she had told a wheelchair bound 90-year-old man suffering from dementia, 'Don't you f**k about with me.' Other serious allegations included instructing two care assistants not to lift a 78-year-old man with dementia after he had fallen on the floor with his trousers around his ankles and was bleeding from a head wound. At a re-opened hearing, the NMC conduct committee decided that the nurse, who for ten years had trained other nurses, had acted in a way that amounted to professional misconduct. The panel decided to issue a caution, which would remain on her records for five years.

30 July 2003
A care home manager has been struck off the nursing register after being found guilty of hitting, dragging and roughly treating frail, elderly residents. It was alleged that the nurse pulled their hair, slapped and pushed them, ignored their injuries and shouted at patients when they did not keep quiet. The committee found 25 out of 32 allegations had been proved from the evidence of other nurses and care assistants.

FINANCIAL ABUSE
Includes stealing or defrauding someone of goods, money, pension book or property.

15 October 2003
A senior care home worker admitted systematically plundering a resident's bank account of more than £12,000. The carer pleaded guilty to six specimen charges of theft and asked for a further 41 similar counts to be taken into consideration.

22 October 2003
A woman who had been employed as a home help by the council for a sheltered housing complex abused her trust by stealing from two of the residents. She stole £150 from a 72-year-old woman and £250 from an 81-year-old man. Her pleas of 'not guilty' to stealing £80 from another flat in the complex and stealing £100 and items from another flat were accepted.

SEXUAL ABUSE
Includes forcing someone to participate in sexual actions or conversation of a sexual nature against their wishes.

16 September 2003
A care home nurse who was struck off the nursing register in July 2001 for making lewd suggestions to elderly residents will not be allowed back into the profession. At the time, he admitted five allegations of misconduct and the committee heard how he acted inappropriately, gyrating his hips against the body of a resident and touching her buttocks.

6 August 2003
A nurse who molested ten helpless women patients when they were too ill to complain was struck off the nursing register. Many of the women were in their 80s and were unable to defend themselves or report the attacks because of their ailments. On 5 December 2002, a jury convicted the nurse of ten charges of indecent assault and he was jailed for three years.

NEGLECT
Includes failing to provide food, heat, clothing, appropriate medical attention (leading, for example, to bed sores) or other things essential to physical and mental well-being.

the result of the introduction of adult protection policies within each local authority area (again leading to increased awareness and reporting) or it may be the result of other factors. AEA has heard concerns expressed by some practitioners that it may be an actual increase in abuse itself, caused by serial abusers moving from childcare environments (where there are increased controls and vigilance) to adult care environments that are less regulated.

While there is no statistical evidence to support these concerns, it is the case that such abuse can be perpetrated not for sexual gratification but to satisfy the urge to control and dominate. *'Sexual offenders are attracted by the vulnerability and availability of their potential victims and those who suffer from physical and mental impairment may be especially at risk'* (Glendenning 1999). Consequently, it is important to note that sexual violence affects older women as well as those who are younger.

NEGLECT

Neglect was formally recognised as a category of abuse in *No Longer Afraid* (Department of Health 1993) and reiterated in *No Secrets* (Department of Health 2000b) reflecting the requirements of the Human Rights Act 1998. However, criminal prosecutions do not appear to have been readily forthcoming, even where the level of neglect by care staff has been extreme.

A number of arguments are commonly cited as to why the criminal law is little used in elder abuse and neglect cases. These include the need for a good prospect of conviction and the requirement that prosecution is in the public interest. A high standard of proof is required and there is a preference for oral evidence. Currently, it appears that older people are not often considered

for special support under the vulnerable witnesses processes.

One of the most common indicators of neglect that comes to our attention relates to the incidence of pressure or bed sores. *'Also called pressure ulcers (death of skin and underlying tissues from the effect of pressure, friction and shear), these are a quality indicator and the development of pressure sores implies neglect'* (Bennett 2003). *'The magnitude of this condition is illuminating … with approximately 10 per cent of hospital inpatients developing pressure ulcers'* (O'Dea 1999). A consistent theme of calls to the helpline, however, is the apparent failure by investigators to consider pressure sores with the degree of seriousness that the above statements imply.

There also appears to be a lack of general knowledge relating to circumstances in which a member of the public can be considered to have assumed a duty of care under case law (R vs Stone & Dobinson [1977] 2 All ER 341) and consequently charged for any failings in that regard. Although this option has been available for 30 years, it has not been used, perhaps because the law deals more readily with acts of commission rather than omission.

In the case law in question, however, it was recognised that a crime was capable of commission by omission, where duty of care had been assumed. The case involved a couple who had assumed the care of a relative who later died in appalling circumstances, severely emaciated and with infected bed sores and other problems. Both defendants were convicted of negligent manslaughter.

FINANCIAL ABUSE

Financial abuse occurs in 10 to 15 per cent of cases involving registered enduring powers

of attorney, and more often with unregistered powers. Expressed as a percentage this may seem to be a relatively minor problem, but 10,000 powers will be registered with the Court of Protection this year alone and frauds involving six-figure sums are by no means unprecedented.
(Lush 1999)

Of all the calls to the helpline regarding financial abuse, the misuse of unregistered powers of attorney continues to be one of the greatest concerns. The ease with which abusers are apparently able to convince older people that an unregistered power of attorney has conveyed a level of financial – and other – control to the abuser is worrying. This is particularly so, given that it is impossible to quantify how many of these unregistered documents are actually in the community.

A predominant theme that emerges from calls to the helpline relating to financial abuse by families is a relative's expectation that they will inherit the bulk of an older person's estate and their consequent desire to preserve as much of that estate as possible.

6 Who are the abusers?

Gender and related factors

In gender terms, more men are reported to us as individual abusers (41 per cent) than women (25 per cent). Overwhelmingly, male abusers are family members (64 per cent). But while this is equally true for women (51 per cent) there is also a significant proportion (33 per cent) of female abusers identified as paid staff.

It is particularly worth noting that, in a third of circumstances, the abuse is perpetrated by more than one person in collusion.

Although 23 per cent of this 'collusive' abuse is perpetrated by family members, a staggering 62 per cent is perpetrated by paid staff – that is, through abusive practices that are institutional and passed from one worker to another. This gives us two messages, the first being a negative one about the quality of formal care. But the second message is that this form of abuse can be addressed by culture change and training. It has the potential to be prevented.

Relationship of abusers to victims

The majority of abusers are related to their victim (46 per cent), with paid workers being the next highest category (34 per cent).

A major point to note, however, is that we are unable to support the hypothesis that the stress of unpaid/family caring leads to abusive practices. While it is accepted that such caring can be intensely stressful, we receive less than one per cent of calls identifying these carers as abusers. Instead, from a domestic violence perspective, it is sons and daughters first (50 per cent) and then partners (23 per cent) who abuse.

This information from the helpline tends to support the conclusions of the 1990 Homer and Gilleard research into abuse by carers. It suggests that physical and verbal abuse has less to do with the condition of the person who is abused and more to do with their family and living situation. That is to say, the factors giving rise to the abuse stem from household circumstances and relationships and personalities rather than from conditions common to ageing such as immobility, incontinence and dementia (Amiel and Heath 2003).

Verbal abuse and neglect but not physical abuse were associated with a poorer premorbid relationship with the patient. Carers who admitted to verbal abuse noted frequent arguments with the patient as a feature of their interactions with the patient before the onset of dementia. (Cooney and Mortimer 1995).

The fact is that large numbers of carers are under stress but do not abuse their relatives.

The groups of relatives who are identified as abusers are:

Type	%
Son/daughter	50
Sibling	3
In-law	9
Partner	23
Parent	1
Niece/nephew	2
Other	11

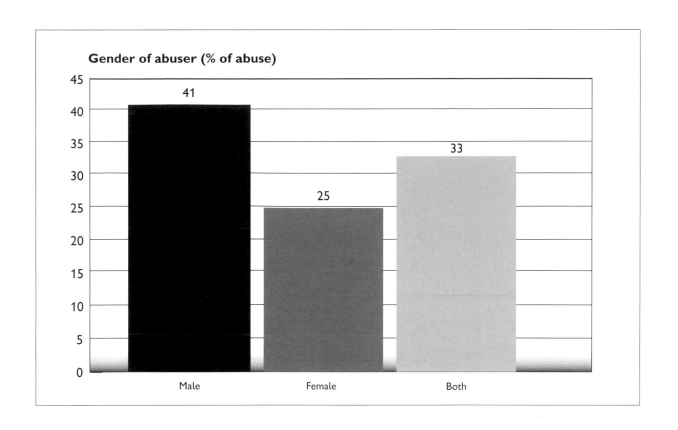

Gender of abuser (% of abuse)

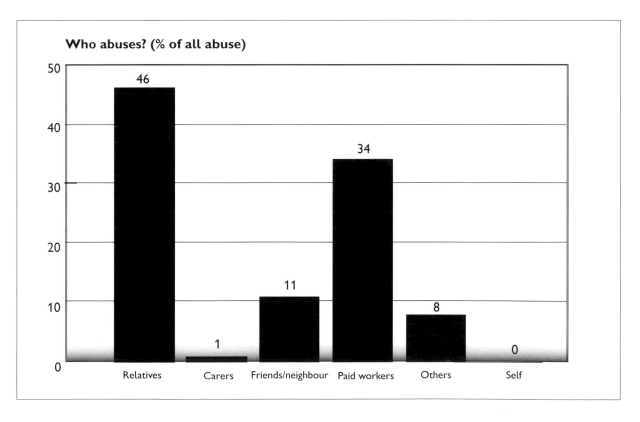

Who abuses? (% of all abuse)

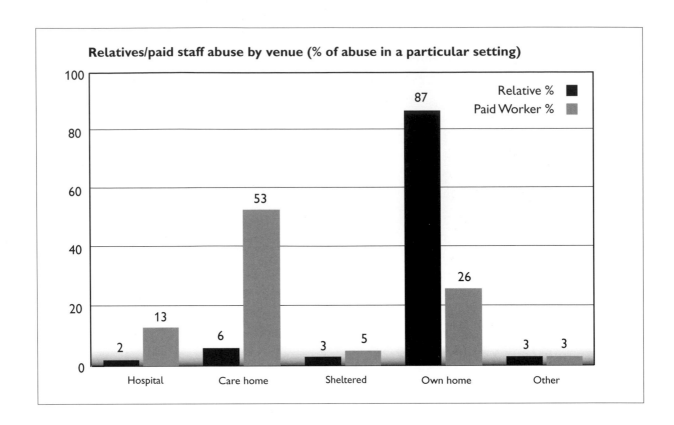

Relatives/paid staff abuse by venue (% of abuse in a particular setting)

The types of paid staff who are identified as abusers are:

Type	% of calls
Care worker (residential and domiciliary)	49
Nurse	11
Social worker	5
Hospital doctor	3
General practitioner	3
Housing worker	5
Legal services	2
Police	1

Not surprisingly, abuse by relatives occurs primarily within the victim's own home (87 per cent) with 6 per cent occurring within care homes. Paid staff are identified as primarily abusing within care homes (53 per cent) as opposed to the victim's own home (26 per cent). However, as the majority of older people receive support from paid staff within

their own homes, this percentage is worryingly high.

Reports of abuse by nurses relate first to hospitals (51 per cent) and then to what were formerly known as nursing homes but are now included in the category of care homes (37 per cent).

7 Who are the victims?

Gender

The vast majority of those who are reported as suffering abuse are women (67 per cent) with 22 per cent of men identified as victims. In a smaller percentage of cases (11 per cent) both men and women are facing abuse at the same time, and half of these (50 per cent) are in some form of institution, primarily care homes.

The fact that more women than men are identified as suffering abuse is likely to reflect the reality that women live longer than men and are consequently more likely to be living alone. *'The majority of men of all ages in the UK live with a partner but vastly larger numbers of women, particularly over the age of 80, live on their own'* (McCreadie 1996). It is their circumstances that make women vulnerable in such situations, not their gender.

It is also necessary to note that men are less likely to report being abused. *'Because of their adherence to social expectations, it is likely that many men do not disclose the abuse they suffer; therefore, the real prevalence is likely to be much higher than is acknowledged either by victims or by the services'* (Pritchard 2001).

Age

More than three-quarters of abuse reported to the helpline (78 per cent) is perpetrated against people who are over the age of 70, with 16 per cent of that abuse affecting people over the age of 90.

In terms of the total number of people, both male and female, identified as victims through the helpline, the following table demonstrates their age range.

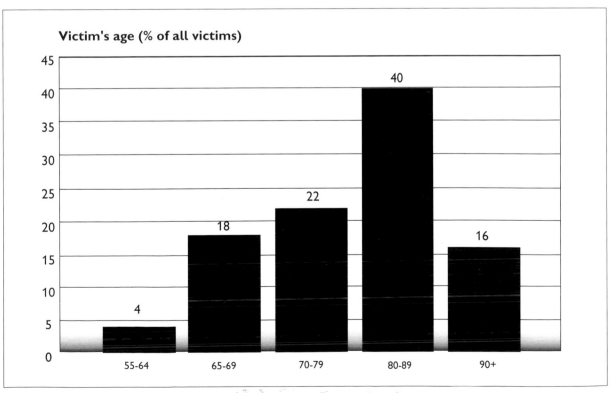

Victim's age (% of all victims)

Age range	%
55-64	4
65-69	18
70-79	22
80-89	40
90+	16

Age range	Male %	Female %
55 to 64	4.8	4.2
65 to 69	18.3	17.7
70 to 79	20.1	22.9
80 to 89	39.5	39.2
90+	17.2	16.0

For both men and women, it appears that the period between 80 and 89 years of age is the time of most vulnerability to abuse.

8 Settings of abuse

Where abuse occurs

Most abuse reported to the helpline occurs in people's own homes (64 per cent). This is not surprising as it is where the majority of older people live and where it is very difficult to monitor and confirm the level of poor practice or relationships.

However, 23 per cent of reports to the helpline concern care homes (formerly known as residential and nursing homes), where less than five per cent of the older population live. Only four per cent of people in Great Britain over retirement age (65 years) live in a care setting (ONS 1999). This is a disproportionate figure, made starker by the reality that callers need to be able to access a telephone in private – something that is not always easy in a care home. They may also have few visitors who can take action on their behalf or they may have physical or mental disabilities that make using a telephone difficult (for example, hearing or speech impairment or a learning disability). Moreover, the very real fear expressed by family members is that complaining about abuse in a care setting may lead to retribution.

In this context, it is worth noting that care homes generally provide services to highly dependent people. *'Overall 57 per cent of women and 48 per cent of men in care homes had a severe personal care disability, that is, needed assistance with one or more self-care tasks, compared with 4 per cent of men and 2 per cent of women living in private households. Assistance with dressing was the most common need, followed by help with using the toilet, transfer from bed or chair, washing and feeding. For each self-care task, higher proportions of women than men needed assistance'* (Department of Health 2000a).

Hospital settings account for 5 per cent of all calls while sheltered housing

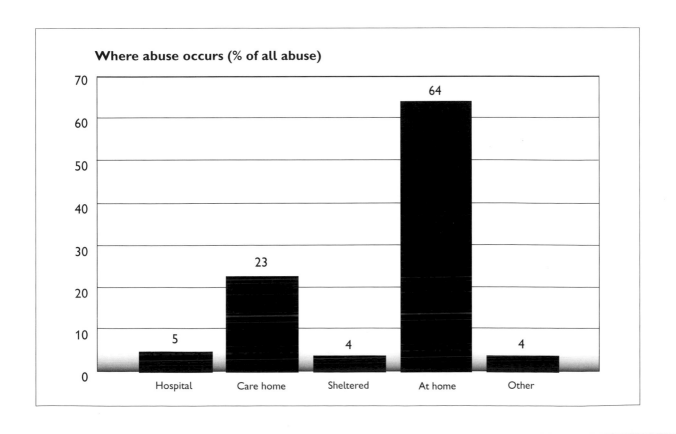

Where abuse occurs (% of all abuse)

Setting	%
Hospital	5
Care home	23
Sheltered	4
At home	64
Other	4

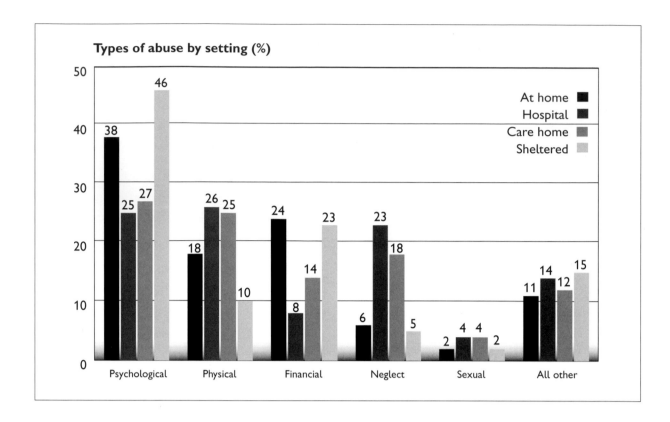

Types of abuse by setting (%)

Legend:
- At home ■
- Hospital ■
- Care home ■
- Sheltered □

Type	At home	Hospital	Care home	Sheltered
Psychological	38	25	27	46
Physical	18	26	25	10
Financial	24	8	14	23
Neglect	6	23	18	5
Sexual	2	4	4	2
All other	11	14	12	15

accounts for 4 per cent. With regard to hospitals, we believe that this is an under-reporting, which can be attributed in part to the nature of the environment that does not readily give control to the patient.

Abuse varies with the setting

Analysis of the types of abuse that occur in individual settings indicates that it is to some degree dependent upon environmental factors. For example, the incidence of psychological abuse is greater in sheltered housing (46 per cent) and at home (38 per cent) than it is in care homes (27 per cent) or hospitals (25 per cent).

However, the incidence of physical abuse is greater in hospitals (26 per cent) and care homes (25 per cent) than it is at home (18 per cent) or in sheltered housing (10 per cent).

The incidence of financial abuse mirrors

that of psychological abuse – it is greater in sheltered housing (23 per cent) and at home (24 per cent) than it is in care homes (14 per cent) or hospitals (8 per cent).

The incidence of neglect mirrors that of physical abuse – it is greater in hospitals (23 per cent) and care homes (18 per cent) than it is at home (6 per cent) or in sheltered housing (5 per cent).

The percentages of sexual abuse are too small to quantify.

Put simply, therefore, it is possible to suggest that financial and psychological abuses could be associated with domiciliary settings while physical abuse and neglect could be associated with institutions.

Within a domiciliary environment, it is predominantly relatives who perpetrate abuse. However, 26 per cent of abusers are care workers and 10 per cent are nurses.

Abuse by paid workers within the home setting is as follows:

Psychological	35%
Physical	12%
Financial	37%
Neglect	15%
Sexual	1%

9 The four nations

Although the majority of calls to the helpline continue to be from England, there is growing contact from the three other nations within the UK, and from the Republic of Ireland.

This could be attributed in part to the development of adult protection or elder abuse initiatives (for example, In Safe Hands in Wales and Elder Abuse projects within the Republic) but it may also be as a consequence of increased publicity about AEA in newspapers, and on television and radio.

From the perspective of responding to sensitive personal issues such as elder abuse, we believe that it is very important to consider and understand the background, history and culture of people in order to provide appropriate support. As a result, we have begun to analyse helpline data to extract information about the various nations. It is worth noting, however, that the total numbers are relatively small and so only limited conclusions may be drawn.

Nation	Number of calls
Scotland	549
Wales	280
Northern Ireland	138
Republic of Ireland	138

In terms of total population, the contact from Northern Ireland represents a greater proportion than that from the Republic.

There is clear evidence of multiple incidents of abuse (for example, the 280 calls about abuse in Wales related to 428 incidents of abuse) although this was less apparent in Ireland as a whole, where numbers remained consistent.

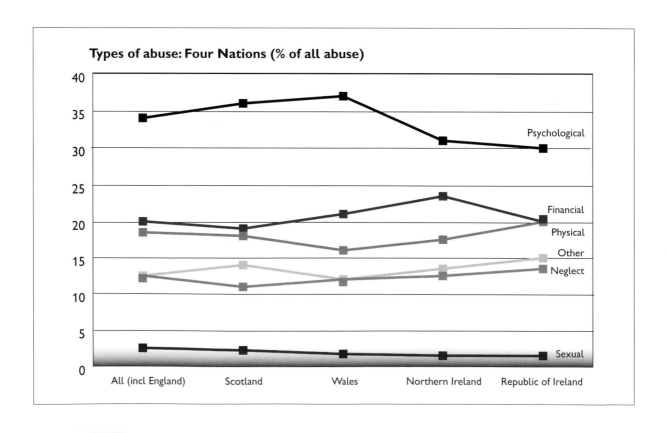

Types of abuse: Four Nations (% of all abuse)

Nation	Abuse incidents
Scotland	836
Wales	428
Northern Ireland	199
Republic of Ireland	199

However, when the data is analysed to ascertain types of abuse, perpetrators and victims, some variations and differences begin to emerge.

For example, while psychological abuse continues to be the primary type of abuse perpetrated against older people throughout the UK and the Republic, there is some slight variation when compared with other types of abuse. Psychological abuse represents 37 per cent of all abuse within Wales and 36 per cent in Scotland but only 31 per cent of all abuse in Northern Ireland and 30 per cent in the Republic of Ireland.

Interestingly, there appears to be greater variation between the incidence of physical and financial abuse within Wales and Northern Ireland than is apparent in Scotland or the Republic of Ireland.

Overwhelmingly, victims are women throughout the nations but there are some slight variations, with Wales showing fewer instances of both men and women being abused simultaneously (7 per cent compared with a mean of 10 per cent). Scotland had the highest levels of this type of 'dual' abuse (12 per cent).

There are no unusual variations in terms of where abuse occurs. Abuse within the victim's own home continues to be the primary location, followed by care homes, hospitals, sheltered housing and then other settings.

While the percentage of calls relating to care home abuse has increased overall from 21 per cent in 2000 to 23 per cent in 2003, there are some slight national differences – 22 per cent in the Republic, 21 per cent in Scotland, and 20 per cent in both Wales and Northern Ireland.

There are some differences when abuse is considered from a domestic violence perspective. While the primary family abusers continue to be the son or daughter followed by the partner, abuse by in-laws shows some variation (shown as a percentage of all abuse).

In-laws	%
All	9
Scotland (SC)	5
Wales (WA)	14
Northern Ireland (NI)	14
Republic of Ireland (IRL)	4

There also appear to be some variations with regard to the age of victims, with Wales showing a slightly higher percentage of victims in the 80 to 89 group and Northern Ireland showing a similar picture for those over 90.

Percentages	Mean	ALL	SC	WA	NI	IRL
Psychological	34	34	36	37	31	30
Physical	18	19	18	16	18	20
Financial	21	20	19	21	24	20
Neglect	12	12	11	12	13	14
Sexual	2	3	2	2	2	2
Other	13	13	14	12	14	15

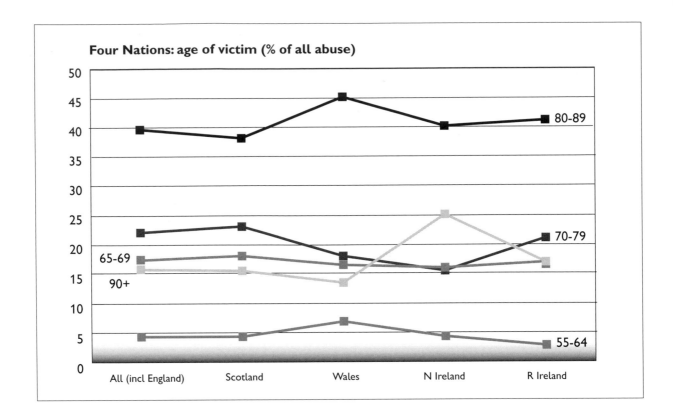

Four Nations: age of victim (% of all abuse)

There are no differences across the nations in terms of primary abusers – a consistent pattern emerges of relatives (but not the 'hands-on' carer) followed by paid workers. Obvious differences, however, relate to a higher percentage of paid workers identified as abusers in Wales (36 per cent of total identified abusers compared to a mean of 32 per cent) and a higher percentage of friends/neighbours identified as abusers in Northern Ireland (16 per cent of total identified abusers compared to a mean of 11 per cent).

We may not be able to draw meaningful conclusions from any of these national differences because of the small numbers involved. However, we believe they may be worth exploring in more detail in the future.

10 Perceptions that influence our understanding of abuse

Concepts of crime and ageing

There are a number of important issues to consider concerning the concept of elder abuse.

The first is to recognise that many of these abuses could also be considered crimes — theft, assault, neglect, rape, breach of the Human Rights Act. By classifying them as something different, there is a real danger of diminishing the impact of the acts themselves, and thereby lessening the importance of the older victim in comparison with younger age groups. As a society, we do not view the assault of a 90-year-old in the same way as an assault on a 30-year-old. This is partly about perceptions of ageing but it also relates to why the older person was assaulted.

Regardless of age, every person is entitled to the protection of basic human rights. We therefore support the arguments made by Help the Aged that: *'the necessary safeguarding of human rights, particularly those protected under Articles 2 (the right to life), 3 (to protection from inhuman and degrading treatment), and 8 (the right to respect for private and family life) must be secured by the positive actions of the State if they cannot be protected by individual redress'* (Harding and Gould 2003).

To put this in context, where acts of elder abuse are actually prosecutable crimes in law, it would be worth considering how often they are actually viewed as crimes in reality, and how many people are prosecuted. In avoiding or ignoring the issue of criminality, there is a danger of colluding in the discrimination against older people, leaving them outside the protection of ordinary civil and human rights. In short, while many protective concepts within social policy are necessarily applicable to elder abuse (and there is much to learn from the fields of domestic violence, child protection and learning disability) there are also differences, not least because of the inevitability of ageing and increased vulnerability.

There are many derogatory terms used about older people: 'senile', 'crumbly', 'wrinkly', 'gaga', 'old git', and 'geriatric'. But as Norman pointed out in her paper on ageism in 1987, *'We don't call a sick child a paediatric, or a woman having a hysterectomy an obstetric'*. She went on to declare that the words used about older age were invariably infantilising: 'old folk', 'old girls', and 'second childhood' (quoted in Glendenning 1997).

It is this derogatory approach to the individual older person that translates into the global view of a group who are burdensome within society. As Chris Phillipson (1998) argued, ageing has been seen as an increasing problem since the birth of the welfare state — enforced retirement, 'elderly medicines', the loss of 'self' into a homogenous group of 'elderly', and an increasing dependency that *'increases the burden on the hard-working, non-elderly population'*. Phillipson and others argue that this belief is not borne out by research, which shows that few older people ever require or use the welfare system.

However, the 'construction' of older people as both dependent and a burden implies that society has developed a feeling that all people aged over 65 need care. And by nurturing the idea of such a dependent (and growing) population, we as a society make older people much more vulnerable.

The challenge is to see beyond individual prejudices and to recognise that dependency is often enforced. We should therefore seek to work in ways that empower people to take control over their own future and not infantilise them (Hockey 1993).

Understanding abuse

The second issue to consider is what we actually mean by abuse. For example, can someone who punches their 80-year-old, disabled grandparent be placed in the same category as the care worker who forgets to knock on a resident's door before entering?

Clearly, the first scenario is grounded in the idea of 'intent to inflict harm', and the concepts of abuse or assault fit relatively easily. The second is perhaps less clear as it is less likely that the care worker intends to inflict harm. It is this second category that is often described as 'poor practice'.

We believe that this is about concepts of dependency. If the resident does not complain about the behaviour, it does not mean that it is not abuse. There is a need to look at how behaviour is experienced by the recipient (in this case the resident) in order to understand whether the practice is abusive. Would you want to be treated in that way? Would the resident choose to be treated in that way if he or she were able-bodied and could have a greater say in the intervention that is occurring? If the answer to these questions is no, then the practices could well be abusive, and in effect could also constitute an assault or intimidation, as in the first scenario.

We have already outlined the five categories usually used to describe different types of abuse. But the overall definitions also need to include an understanding of institutional abuse along with an awareness of institutional racism. This is where individual institutions employ regimes that are essentially abusive in nature as well as environments that are systematically abusive in their treatment, including ageist and racist.

This institutional abuse is graphically illustrated by the case of Nye Bevan Lodge, a local authority home in Southwark, South London, where *'elderly, often confused residents were made to eat their own faeces, left unattended, physically manhandled, forced to pay money to care staff and even helped to die'* (Vousden 1987).

Taking a client-centred perspective (as proposed in the National Service Framework for Older People) immediately helps to reinforce the importance of the individual instead of relying on preconceived 'norms' and notions about older people in general. We believe this brief sentence conveys the issue most poignantly: *'Beginning to see elders as objects rather than human is the foundation on which a continuum of petty slights and abuses build into active mistreatment'* (Biggs, Phillipson and Kingston 1995).

The citizenship of victims

Increasingly, social care policy is drawing attention to the need to place independent living and the protection of older people within a citizenship framework. By doing so, prevention, protection and support become part of the wider intentions of community planning, including social inclusion, crime and disorder, regeneration and neighbourhood renewal. Such a shift in policy focus is in line with the implicit messages in *No Secrets* (Department of Health 2000b).

Rather than regarding vulnerable older people primarily as clients and patients in need of protection, citizenship *'seeks to reinforce the mutual obligations (between individual and society) inherent in social inclusion policies'*.

But we also need regulation to mirror this change in strategic direction and to reframe standards to include not only

effective engagement but also how far patients, residents and clients exercise control over their own lives. Such regulation needs to encourage organisations to have staffing regimes and cultures underpinned by and through citizenship empowerment.

In partnership with Better Government for Older People (BGOP), AEA began exploring community-based and community-led approaches in 2003. We expect this work to demonstrate the necessity for joined-up governance at local, national and UK levels.

11 Theoretical models and risk factors

Academics and practitioners have identified certain predisposing factors within any abusive situation. In 1997, for example, Bennett et al looked at the five most-cited risk factors and their effectiveness in determining that abuse is occurring. We briefly describe these risk factors.

Intra-individual dynamics

Many previous studies had shown that a history of alcohol dependency or mental ill health in a carer were risk factors. Subsequently, however, people questioned what comes first – the stress of caring leading to the use of alcohol or alcohol dependency, making someone less likely to cope with the caring role? This raised doubts about whether this was indeed an effective indicator of abuse.

Penhale, Parker and Kingston (2000) concluded their discussion of risk factors by saying: *'Mental health, alcohol and/or substance misuse [etc] are important factors to consider in a comprehensive assessment. However, it is not possible for practitioners to confidently predict levels of risk of abuse simply by identifying these factors alone.'*

Inter-generational transmission of violence

This considers whether abuse is an extension of domestic violence into older age or whether children of previously abusive parents later turn the violence against their dependent mother or father. Bennett et al found no

evidence of either in their study although this may have been because it is notoriously difficult to penetrate such private aspects of life in a traditional academic way.

Dependency

This tends to be the 'logical' explanation for elder abuse. However, dependency is a multi-tiered and complicated issue which can rarely be taken at face value. Dependency can result from the benefits trap for carers or the degree to which the cared for person needs support. This is certainly a major issue for consideration in any social or health care assessment (including carers' needs assessment).

Stress

A number of people think that the stress of caring automatically leads to abuse but this is far too simplistic an idea to be a major predisposing or risk factor. Indeed, our helpline analysis indicates that only 1 per cent of calls are about abuse perpetrated by a primary carer. Far more likely is that the abuser is a removed relative or a paid worker. This assumption therefore needs to be handled carefully for the sake of both the carer and the cared-for person.

Social isolation

Research has suggested that isolation may well be a predisposing factor for abuse. This is potentially important because 36 per cent of those living in care homes and 19 per cent of those living in private households are rarely visited by relatives or friends, with 6 per cent of care home residents and 2 per cent of those living at home receiving no visits at all (Department of Health 2000a).

It is also possible that the older person is living with someone, even in a communal setting, but that they have few social ties outside that relationship.

Other theories

Pillemer and Finklehor (1989) found that 'abuser deviance' was an important casual factor. They concluded that 'elder abusers appear to be severely troubled individuals with histories of anti-social behaviour or instability'.

Mervyn Eastman highlighted the influence of pathological family cultures as a cause of violence and cruelty by abusive family members (Eastman 1984).

Research by McCreadie et al (2000) sought to predict a 'diagnosis' of abuse by GPs in two locations. GPs were seven times more likely to have identified a case of physical or verbal abuse or neglect if they had also identified patients in five or more risk situations for abuse. The most commonly identified risk situations involved alcohol consumption, dementia and problems of a household member, including problems of the carer.

In 1988, Roger Clough produced a list of factors that could indicate a predisposition toward abuse in institutions: 'There have been a series of complaints over a long period, relating to more than one member of staff; the establishment is run-down and basic arrangements for laundry and hygiene are poor, for example a pervasive smell of urine; there are staff shortages and staff sickness; senior staff are on holiday; there is little supervision of staff and they are able to develop their own patterns of work (we know little of what happens at night-time); staff have been in charge of the unit for a considerable period of time; there is a high turnover of staff; staff drink alcohol regularly during breaks or when on duty; there is uncertainty about the future of the establishment; there are few visitors; residents are highly dependent on staff for personal care; residents go out little or have few contacts; a particular resident has no one taking an active interest in him or her; there is discord among the staff team or between staff and managers; the residents are troublesome, when their care makes heavy demands or when the task to be carried out is unpleasant.'

Finally, Whittaker (1997) has suggested that abuse between two people can occur only if a power imbalance exists between them – one person perceives himself and is perceived by the other as being more powerful while the other perceives himself and is perceived as being relatively powerless. These perceptions are not necessarily conscious but are derived from the detailed routines of daily life and the establishment of patterns of interaction that confirm and reinforce the individuals' relative positions of power.

However, the problem with any list of risk factors is that it is rarely comprehensive, so the aim should always be to ask questions about the lives, support needs and choices of the individuals involved. In other words, just because someone lives alone and has a daughter with long-term mental health problems as a carer does not automatically indicate a predisposition towards abuse. Similarly, someone displaying behaviour that is not on the list of indicators could still be a victim or an abuser.

The premise of good adult protection needs to be that information, behaviour or clues should not be judged simply on the basis of 'tick boxes', prejudices or assumptions. The aim should be to draw together the information surrounding the

individual concerned, within the context
of their life and relationships, and within
the boundaries of the policy and
procedure of any particular authority.

12 Successful interventions

Underlying principles

In considering successful intervention strategies, we believe that it is necessary to start from the premise that prevention is always better than intervention. We believe that this approach should be inherent in adult protection policies and procedures because the reality of protective work is very often about reducing the potential for abuse rather than stopping the act itself.

Adopting this approach is important because the dynamics of elder abuse can be similar to those within domestic violence settings – the victim may be unable to perceive himself/herself as such and therefore may be unable to accept the options for escape or protection that are immediately available. It is crucial that practitioners are taught to switch to preventative work rather than concluding that nothing can be done and closing the case. While it might not be possible to provide protection to the older person at that moment, it might be possible to work towards providing protection in six months' time, once the practitioner has gained the victim's confidence and helped them to recognise and accept the options available to them.

Collaborative working

Successful adult protection requires multi-layered strategies that operate simultaneously. It also needs co-ordination between agencies; the sharing of information; and a willingness to seek expert advice from others.

This invariably involves strong leadership from the top down; co-ordination between practitioners; liaison that keeps the older person at the centre of planning; and empowerment. None of this is complex but all of it requires resistance to pressures that can be intense – heavy caseloads; budget and time constraints; resource and training difficulties; and the temptation to see an older person's refusal of help as an opportunity to close the case, or evict, or ignore.

Developing unique strategies

It is not appropriate simply to import child protection strategies into adult protection because they may not necessarily work. Adults with capacity have choice, and while they may be frail and vulnerable, they have the right to exercise that choice and control as they wish. It is therefore important to take what is appropriate from the experiences of other abuse scenarios and then tailor it to meet the needs of adults.

A good example of how strategies may not easily translate to this field would be to consider 'places of safety'. In child protection, this can be a ready option to ensure the security of a vulnerable child. But with an older adult, such a strategy might be disastrous. Not only might a move be severely traumatic for the victim, even fatal, but it may also be the very thing that the abuser wants – for example, to gain possession of the family home.

So we need to think creatively about this area of adult protection and do much more work to develop unique strategies. These will emerge clearly only after practitioners have received quality training, gained greater expertise in the field, and had the opportunity to share their experiences and learn from each other.

Addressing poor practice

TRAINING

The experience of the AEA helpline is that poor practice forms the greatest percentage of abuse perpetrated by paid staff. Consequently, we strongly promote training as one guaranteed method of reducing the potential for such abuse.

This approach has been informed by research in both America and the UK, which indicates that training can directly impact upon levels of abuse. In 1988 and 1991, Pillemer conducted research into abuse in nursing homes. The quality of care was better in homes that could afford to hire staff with sound training and where staff/patient ratios were relatively high. Nurses and nursing aides with lower levels of training and education were likely to have more negative attitudes towards older people (Pillemer 1988). British research has subsequently confirmed this conclusion (Baillon et al 1996).

Care staff need training in how to provide quality care. Increasing numbers of experienced social and health care staff are beginning to question strategies that rely either on theory, without practical training in caring techniques, or that do not, in reality, constitute training at all. National Vocational Qualifications, for example, assess current skills and knowledge but do not develop new practical skills.

It is not only care staff who need the right training, however, but also other groups throughout the sector, including inspectors and investigators.

Regulatory inspectors in social and health care need training appropriate to the services they are inspecting, so, for example, an inspector of   care homes providing nursing should have a good knowledge of nursing practice. But they also need training in understanding what constitutes abuse; what are unacceptable thresholds that warrant enforcement action; how their role should integrate with adult protection policies, and how to focus on outcomes instead of processes.

Investigators need training in how to investigate; what options can be considered when seeking solutions, and what legislation can be used to progress protection.

And abuse training needs to be integrated into the professional programmes for nurses, doctors (including GPs), pharmaceutical advisers in Primary Care Trusts and so on. We believe that it is only by making adult protection training an integral part of mainstream development that the scale of the problem can be effectively challenged.

CULTURE

We believe that the culture of an organisation can encourage abuse. In our experience, it is not linked to low pay – there are many poorly paid staff providing excellent care. But if boundaries are not maintained and reinforced, this can lead to abuse. For example, the care worker who casually barges into a resident's room without knocking is breaking through a boundary. Once that becomes the norm without being challenged by managers or peers, the next boundary is ready to be breached, and so on until a very serious incident occurs.

So culture is important and that can be affected only by good training and good supervision, and setting realistic standards, monitoring them and reacting accordingly. Such reactions should not just be about punitive action. The provider who is maintaining a quality environment and responding to an abusive staff member needs access to good advice and guidance, and that support should be available from the relevant regulator.

We also need to develop a general culture that is not restricted by professional boundaries but that encourages practitioners to seek other opinions and advice. We need to create a climate where it is acceptable to question and challenge without repercussions. We need to prevent secrecy, not encourage it, because the abuser thrives in secrecy. And we need to address the failures in whistle-blowing (see opposite).

EMPOWERMENT

We also need to look closely at what constitutes genuine empowerment. Research into adult protection in England at the beginning of 2003 showed that the vast majority of local authorities had met their statutory responsibility in enabling procedures (97 per cent). But they had failed miserably to publicise the existence of those procedures (Centre for Policy on Ageing 2003). Less than 2 per cent had invested in systems to tell people about adult protection.

This raises a basic question – what value is a human right if you do not know about it or cannot access it?

People need to be able to make informed choices, without pressure, without coercion, and without the advice-giver having any secondary

loyalties. There is a real danger that decisions are taken 'in the best interests' of the victim but without their consent.

We must not infantilise older adults in this way. It is all too easy where there is doubt about someone's capacity to make decisions. But if we take away someone's right to make a decision or fail to identify what they would have wanted – and we do it in the name of protection – then we run the risk of becoming abusers ourselves.

WHISTLE-BLOWING

The current reality of whistle-blowing in social or health care is that it challenges individual security and relationships, and serves to identify only certain types of abuse. Moreover, it is only staff who are seen as legitimate whistle-blowers. Residents, service users or relatives are often not perceived to possess the status, expertise or professionalism, and are seen instead as complainants or witnesses.

Whistle-blowing has another characteristic. It appears to be 'worth it' only if the abuse or neglect is so blatant that an individual feels it is worth paying the price of any repercussions (Manthorpe and Stanley 1999).

We believe that whistle-blowing can be a crucial component in strategies to combat abuse. But this will happen only when whistle-blowing itself becomes integrated into the wider philosophies of good practice, codes of conduct and expected activities – that is, when professional bodies perceive a failure to 'blow the whistle' as an unacceptable breach of their codes of conduct.

13 About research: a context for the helpline

The robustness of research evidence and potential shortcomings

There has been only one study on the community prevalence of elder abuse in the UK (Ogg and Bennett 1992). To overcome some of the difficulties encountered with research methodology a routine social survey was used – the Office of Population Censuses and Surveys (OPCS) Omnibus survey. This was a representative sampling survey that took place in 100 different sites throughout Britain during May 1992, involving 2,130 adults (593 aged over 60 years and 1,366 people who were in regular close contact with an older person). The survey excluded older people in institutions and those who were too ill or disabled to participate. This is an important limitation, as it excluded some older people who may have been at greater risk of abuse, and certainly at greater risk of harm from any given abuse.

Three categories of abuse were surveyed – physical, oral and financial. Oral abuse (which is categorised by AEA within psychological abuse) was measured by asking whether a close family member or relative had recently frightened them by shouting, insulting them or speaking roughly to them. Physical abuse was measured by asking whether any close family member had pushed, slapped, shoved or been physically rough with them in any other way. The questions about financial abuse asked whether any close family member had taken money or property from them without their consent.

Of the 593 people aged 60 or more who were surveyed, 5 per cent reported having been orally abused, 2 per cent reported physical abuse and 2 per cent financial abuse. The study did not identify the extent of multiple abuses and did not identify the timeframe involved in these abuses. It also included questions to 1,366 people who were in regular close contact with an older person, using the same abuse criteria. This indicated higher rates of oral abuse (9 per cent) but a lower rate for physical abuse (0.6 per cent). There has not been a replication of this study and attempts to conduct large-scales studies of such aspects as risk factors (an attempt to repeat North American work in order to see if the findings were relevant to the UK) have not received funding support.

While some of the research difficulties were overcome by this approach, the study was nevertheless limited in scope. It remains, however, the only indicator of the potential scale of elder abuse within the UK, and is mirrored by research in other countries into percentages of abuse within their older populations, eg Finland 5 per cent, Australia 4.6 per cent, America 3.2 per cent, Canada 4 per cent (O'Loughlin and Duggan 1998).

In the UK, if these percentages were to be applied to the older population living in their own homes, they would indicate that between 5 and 9 per cent of older people were being subjected to oral abuse by family members, equating to between 500,000 and 900,000 people.

More recently, the Community and District Nursing Association (CDNA) published the results of a survey of nurse members in February 2003 (Potter 2003). The survey was conducted during November/December 2002 and the findings of the survey were compiled by the Labour Research Department. Over 700 nurses responded to the survey and the vast majority (88 per cent) indicated that they had encountered elder abuse within their work, while 12 per cent reported that this was on a daily, weekly or monthly basis.

As was noted by a Council of Europe report on Elder Abuse (Council of Europe 1990), the problem common to all European countries is the absence of a policy for monitoring and recording statistics on violence within the family in general and specifically violence against older people.

Overall, therefore, the information available is limited, but taken collectively it implies a level of abuse that is significant.

Until such time as a detailed prevalence study is undertaken into the scope and impact of elder abuse there will remain the potential for individuals and organisations to 'downplay' their beliefs in the scale of the problem, with each having their own motivations in doing so. This is not a position that would be acceptable within the child protection debate. What remains clear, however, is that current primary adult protection initiatives have focused upon services that are provided to older people within institutions or by paid staff, and a strategy has yet to emerge which addresses abuse by families behind closed doors.

About Action on Elder Abuse

Action on Elder Abuse (AEA) is a charity, established in 1993 with the aim of preventing the abuse of older people. It is a membership organisation with more than 500 individual and group members throughout the UK. These include older people, local and national voluntary organisations, academics, health authorities and trusts, and social services departments (often represented by adult protection co-ordinators).

We are seeking an environment in which the abuse of older people is no longer tolerated. We are seeking to encourage public and practitioner recognition of elder abuse, and to facilitate policies, procedures and cultures that both abhor and challenge such abuse.

We believe that it is vital that:

- the existence of elder abuse is recognised and its possible profound effect on the quality of life for older people is understood;

- the rights and autonomy of older people and their possible need to be protected from abuse are recognised;

- all older people have the confidence, knowledge and support to take the action they choose to counter abuse;

- health and social care practitioners at all levels are trained to recognise the different types of abuse and to respond to the needs of both the abused and the abuser;

- health and social service purchasers and providers have staff and services that are responsive to the needs of the abused and the abuser;

- the responses of all statutory, voluntary and independent agencies are collaborative and appropriate; and

- a broad range of research is undertaken to expand our knowledge and understanding of the issues.

Our practical activities include:

- providing up-to-date information for our members;

- running conferences on elder abuse and related issues (including an annual two-day event that brings together academics, practitioners and voluntary sector representatives to consider current developments and challenges);

- providing direct training and facilitating training, as appropriate;

- giving presentations to a wide range of organisations;

- producing leaflets, resource materials and reports for practitioners and the public; and

- acting as a resource for practitioners and all branches of the media.

We also operate the only national confidential helpline service relating to the abuse of older people. The service:

- helps callers identify the options available to them in challenging abuse;

- provides information by letter, telephone or email, for older people themselves, their families and friends among others; and

• helps callers to raise their concerns with statutory bodies.

The service was launched nationally in November 1997 and has now taken more than 10,000 calls, including requests for information.

In addition to providing practical advice to callers, the helpline also provides the only source of national statistical information on the nature of elder abuse, the environments of abuse, and who the abusers and the victims are. This information has been used by academics, researchers and the Department of Health and is also regularly quoted by the media.

We also maintain a press cuttings service and post examples of reported abuse on to our website. On average, 35 examples of abuse are identified each month, almost invariably being reported in local newspapers.

Ultimately, we are working to collectively challenge the societal attitudes described by Holstein in 1996:

'For those who work with abused and neglected older adults, the likelihood of achieving an ideal solution is slim. While the public may be appalled at newspaper descriptions of elder mistreatment, that dismay rarely translates into political action. Despite outrage, few understand the roots of the problem that lead to elder abuse and neglect, and therefore few assume responsibility for activities designed to address these deeper causes. It is unlikely that this picture will change in the immediate future.' (Holstein 1996)

About the Elder Abuse Response helpline

AEA established a pilot helpline in 1995 to provide information on elder abuse and to give support and information to those concerned about specific abuse incidents. A review of the calls received during the pilot year (October 1995 to September 1996) was published in 1997. This demonstrated a clear need for a specialist service on elder abuse for both members of the general public and practitioners in the field. The evaluation's recommendations to expand the service UK-wide were subsequently accepted by the charity's trustees.

The helpline has been operating nationally since 1997 and is run by specially trained staff and volunteers. It is available weekdays between 10.00 am and 4.30 pm on freephone number 0808 808 8141.

The primary limitation of a helpline is that it can give an indication of the nature of abuse only from the perspective of those able (either mentally or physically) and willing to contact a telephone helpline. Abuse often occurs in closed environments – for example, in institutions such as care homes or behind the 'closed doors' of people's own homes. In these settings, victims may not have the means or opportunity to access a helpline. Some callers to our service are in such settings but have temporarily found privacy in which to call, or have left that setting permanently and are able to speak freely. Nevertheless, it is important to remember that there may be significant numbers of victims who could not access the helpline even if they knew about it.

The helpline is publicised as widely as possible through leaflets, posters, information campaigns, word of mouth, and media work. Publicity on national television has the most impact. For example, an undercover report into abuse in care homes (*Who cares for granny?*) broadcast on Channel 5 in October 2003 generated an additional 94 calls to the line. One programme in the *Kilroy* series on BBC1 generated the equivalent of a month of calls in one week.

Unlike individual adult protection committees or co-ordinators who may receive periodic referrals that are complex, the helpline staff receive numerous contacts, so they are well placed to understand the dynamics of elder abuse and appropriate strategies of response. Helpline operators are therefore often used as an expert source by a wide variety of practitioners.

'Elder abuse, like other subjects of public anxiety, is one in which individuals who are affected (in various ways) may seek advice from an expert, anonymised source of help. The nature of contact established through such a helpline is complex: it is not simply a matter of reporting an incident but a dialogue between anonymous voices in which callers decide the level and type of information they are willing to impart. As with other advice lines, it also serves as an information source for those involved in training and education, and also those operating within the arena of adult protection but who feel the need for expert advice and guidance.' (Manthorpe 1999)

References

Action on Elder Abuse/Family Policy Studies Centre (1997) *Hearing the despair: the reality of elder abuse.* London: AEA/Family Policy Studies Centre.

Action on Elder Abuse (2000) *Listening is not enough.* London: AEA.

Amiel, A and I Heath (2003) *Family violence in primary care.*
Oxford: Oxford University Press.

Audit Commission (2003) *Human rights: improving public service delivery.*
London: Audit Commission.

Baillon, S, A Boyle, P G Neville and G Scothern (1996) 'Factors that contribute to stress in care staff in nursing homes for the elderly', *International Journal of Geriatric Psychiatry*, 11: 219-26.

Bennett, G (2003) *Family violence in primary care.*
Oxford: Oxford University Press.

Bennett, G, P Kingston and B Penhale (1997) *The dimensions of elder abuse.*
Basingstoke: Macmillan.

Biggs, S, C Phillipson, and P Kingston, (1995) *Elder abuse in perspective.*
Buckingham: Open University.

Centre for Policy on Ageing (2003) *Research into the implementation of no secrets by local authorities.*
London: CPSA.

Clough, R (1988) 'Danger: look out for abuse', *Care Weekly*, 7.

Cooney, C and A Mortimer (1995) 'Elder abuse and dementia – a pilot study', *International Journal of Social Psychiatry*: 276-83.

Council of Europe (1990) Recommendation No R (90) of the Committee of Ministers to Member States on Social Measures concerning violence within the family. Strasbourg: Council of Europe.

Department of Health (1993) *No longer afraid.* London: HMSO.

Department of Health (2000a) *Health Survey 2000.* London: TSO.

Department of Health (2000b) *No secrets: the protection of vulnerable adults.* Guidance on the development and implementation of multi-agency policies and procedures. London: TSO.

Eastman, M (1984) *Old age abuse.*
London: Age Concern.

Glendenning, F (1997) 'Attitudes to older people' in *The mistreatment of elderly people.* London: SAGE.

Glendenning, F (1999) 'The abuse of older people in institutional settings' in *Institutional abuse.* London: Routledge.

Harding, T and J Gould (2003) *Memorandum on older people and human rights.* London: Help the Aged.

Help the Aged (2004) *Everyday age discrimination: what older people say.* London: Help the Aged

Hockey, J and A James (1993) *Growing up and growing old.* London: Sage.

Holstein, M (1996) 'Multidisciplinary decision-making: uniting differing professional perspectives' in *Elder mistreatment: ethical issues, dilemmas and decisions.* New York: Haworth Press.

Homer, A and C J Gilleard (1990) 'Abuse of older people by their carers', *British Medical Journal*, 301: 1359-62.

Lush, D (1999) 'Taking liberties' in *Bags of money, the financial abuse of older people*. Working Paper No 4. London: AEA.

McCreadie, C (1996) *Elder abuse: update on research*. London: Age Concern Institute of Gerontology, King's College London.

McCreadie, C, G Bennett, M S Gilthorpe, G Houghton and A Tinker (2000) 'Elder abuse: do GPs know or care?', *Journal of the Royal Society of Medicine*, 93(2): 67-72.

Manthorpe, G (1999) 'Putting elder abuse on the agenda: achievements of a campaign' in *Elder abuse – critical issues in policy and practice*.
London: Age Concern.

Manthorpe, J and N Stanley, (1999) 'Shifting the focus, from bad apples to users' rights' in *Institutional abuse*. London: Routledge,

O'Dea, K (1999) 'The prevalence of pressure damage in acute care hospital patients in the UK',
Journal of Wound Care 8(4): 192-4.

Office for National Statistics (1999) *Census* April 1991 and 2001

Ogg J and G Bennett (1992) 'Elder abuse in Britain', *British Medical Journal*, 305: 998-9.

O'Loughlin, A and J Duggan (1998) *Abuse, neglect, mistreatment of older people: an exploratory study*. Dublin: National Council on Ageing and Older People.

Penhale, B, P Parker and P Kingston (2000) *Elder abuse: Practitioners' guide*. London: Venture.

Phillipson, C (1998) *Reconstructing old age*. London: Sage.

Pillemer, K A (1988) 'Maltreatment of patients in nursing homes', *Journal of Health and Social Behaviour*, 29(3): 227-38.

Pillemer, K A and R Bachman-Prehn (1991) 'Helping and hurting: predictors of maltreatment of patients in nursing homes', *Research on Ageing*, 13(1): 74-95.

Pillemer, K and D Finklehor (1989) 'Causes of elder abuse: caregiver stress versus problem relatives', *American Journal of Orthopsychiatry*, Vol 59: 179-87.

Potter, J (2003) *Findings in relation to the Community and District Nursing Association survey examining the issue of elder abuse*. London: CDNA.

Pritchard, J (2001) *Male victims of elder abuse*. London: Jessica Kingsley.

Vousden, M (1987) 'Nye Bevan would turn in his grave', *Nursing Times*, 83: 18-19.

Whittaker, T (1997) 'Rethinking elder abuse: towards an age and gender integrated theory of elder abuse' in *The mistreatment of elderly people*. London: Sage.